A PORTFOLIO OF

WINDOW & WINDOW TREATMENT IDEAS

CONTENTS

COWLES
Creative Publishing, Inc.

President: Iain Macfarlane
Executive V.P./Editor-in-Chief: William B. Jones
Group Director, Book Development: Zoe Graul

Library of Congress
Cataloging-in-Publication Data
A Portfolio of Window & Window Treatment Ideas
p. cm
ISBN 0-86573-956-0 (softcover)
1. Drapery. 2. Windows. 3. Blinds. 4. Window shades.
I. Cy DeCosse Incorporated. II. Title: Portfolio of
windows and window treatment ideas.
TT390.P67 1994
747'.3—dc20   94-36571

Author: Home How-To Institute™
Creative Director: William B. Jones
Project Director: Paul Currie
Art Director: Geoffrey Kinsey
Editor: Carol Harvatin
Project Managers: Carol Harvatin, Tracy Stanley
Copy Editor: Janice Cauley
Production Staff: Amy Berndt, April Jones,
    Geoffrey Kinsey, Julie Sutphen
Vice President of Development
    Planning & Production: Jim Bindas
Production Manager: Linda Halls

Printed by Webcrafters, Inc.
00 99 98 97 / 5 4 3 2 1

WHAT IS THE PERFECT WINDOW?

The perfect window does more than just let light in. The combination of glass and window treatments adds personality and charm to a room's decor as well as shapes and directs light within the room. Windows also contribute toward your indoor comfort by controlling exposure to air and sunlight. In addition, your needs for privacy, energy efficiency and traffic patterns will influence the type, style and placement of the windows and window treatments you choose. This influence includes the visual effect that the windows have on the architectural design of both the interior and the exterior of your home.

Today's windows and window treatments are available in traditional styles and designs, as well as a variety of new styles and combinations, all made with the newest materials and technology. To give you a sample of the wide selection of windows and window treatments available today, *A Portfolio of Window & Window Treatment Ideas* features over 175 color photographs of successful, innovative windows and window treatments at work.

The first part of the book introduces you to the different types and styles of windows and window treatments, and their various features and functions. The second half of the book is a portfolio of dazzling photographs that features all types and styles of windows and window

treatments in creative and dramatic displays. You'll see how different window treatments look on different types of windows, and windows that look sensational with no window treatment at all.

No matter what function a window will have in your home, *A Portfolio of Window & Window Treatment Ideas* is the ideal tool to help you make choices that will meet your needs perfectly.

Three small windows form one large window display over the sink in this contemporary kitchen. The sashes create a geometric design that matches the modern decor. The smallest window is an awning window that can be opened for ventilation.

Walls filled with French doors brighten this formal sunroom setting. The layered arrangement of the curtains and swags adorns the room in tailor-made elegance without looking stuffy.

This expansive window design is composed of casement and fixed windows. The grand scale of the design matches the room size and opens up the interior to the great outdoors.

(above) Simple pleated shades are the perfect treatment for these angled transom windows. The minimal design of the window treatment reinforces the interesting line of the architectural design.

(left) The double-arched design created by the mullions and muntins and the round-top window in this combination give it the characteristics of a Palladian window.

5

PLANNING

Comfort Control

There are a number of strategies for controlling the comfort in your home with windows and window treatments to keep it from gaining heat in the summer and losing heat in the winter.

The most effective way to keep your home cool in hot weather is to block the sun before it has a chance to reach the window. Exterior awnings, canopies, and overhangs keep the sun off the glass without obstructing the view, but they can be costly and aren't always convenient. The easiest way to block the hot sun is to use an interior window treatment.

Unfortunately, many interior window treatments also block the view. But some, like shades and blinds, block out the heat of the sun and still allow air, and some light, to filter through. Blinds with reflective backings tilt to bounce incoming sunlight back out the window.

Heavy draperies, linings and multilayered combinations all insulate windows and inhibit heat loss. Shades that stop air flow reduce heat loss through the glass. One manufacturer uses a magnetic-edge tape on the shade to help seal the edges to the perimeter.

If ventilation is a goal of your window design, make sure to include operable windows like casements, double-hung, sliding, and awning windows. The best windows for ventilation are casement windows; they circulate the most air because the entire window opens.

The changing seasons control the climate in this seasonal porch. The screened walls and roll-up blinds let refreshing breezes blow through on warm summer days. The unobstructed view lets you commune with nature from the comfort of your couch.

A large round-top window catches the sunlight as it moves across the sky throughout the day and heats this upper-story bedroom. To cool the room and circulate air, the two small center windows are casements that can be cranked open to catch a cool breeze.

(above) Round blue awnings stop the hot sunlight before it reaches the windows and keep the inside of the house cool. The cylindrical shape of the awnings complements the rounded contemporary lines of the house.

(left) Sunlight streams into the lofted ceilings of this contemporary living room through the Palladian-style design in a round-top window. A French door is ready to open and usher in fresh air whenever needed.

Awning windows are part of a bow window design that creates this cozy solarium. The two awning windows are located on opposite sides of the space to most effectively draw refreshing scents and breezes into the room.

Photo courtesy of Kolbe & Kolbe Millwork Co.

Summer breezes flow through this poolside cabana when the three sets of French doors are opened. The doors operate independently of each other, so they can be opened as much or as little as desired; or on a cool night they can be closed completely for comfort and privacy.

Photo opposite page courtesy of Marvin Windows

Photo courtesy of Conrad Imports; Design: Marlene Mann; Photography: John Sutton Photography

The climate outside becomes the climate inside when floor-to-ceiling windows and patio doors comprise the walls of a room. Natural Arrowroot sunshades filter enough light to keep the heat out, yet are translucent enough to maintain the open, airy feeling that the generous use of windows gives to the room.

PLANNING

View

When a large window frames an incredible view, it becomes the focal point of a room. Windows with great views shouldn't be cluttered by cumbersome curtains or heavy top treatments. If you want the view to be the center of attention, use a window treatment that doesn't obstruct it. Curtains or drapes that pull back are a good choice. Blinds and shades have a minimal visual impact because they stack up and out of sight when open.

When the view outside isn't so special, the window treatment itself can carry the attention. Interesting fabric styles, colors and patterns or a clever combination of window treatments can be enough to draw attention to the window itself.

Free from any window treatments, this impressive cathedral window arrangement frames a spectacular view that can be enjoyed from anywhere in the room.

A bay window frames a view that looks like a picture postcard. The window seat creates a cozy niche for birdwatching or just counting the clouds.

Floor-to-ceiling windows and overhead skylights expand the room into the lush greenery outside. The view becomes a large part of this room and creates the sensation of being surrounded by foliage.

Photos courtesy of Rushman Industries

The wood slats of these Venetian blinds are finished to match the woodwork in this room. When closed (inset), the wooden slats blend into the woodwork of the room and create a rich, wood-paneled look.

Photo courtesy of Conrad Imports. Design: Shelley Belling. Photo: John Sutton

Translucent natural-fiber shades camouflage the view when closed. The shades operate independently and can be individually adjusted as desired. This shade has been partially opened to create a soft frame for a stunning skyline view. When the shades are open, the large windows bring the skyline panorama so close it becomes a backdrop for the room.

The sweeping geometric design created by the frosted glass in this window also functions as art in this contemporary dining room setting. When light hits the frosted glass, it emphasizes the design. The frosted glass lets in lots of light, but still preserves the room's privacy.

PLANNING

Privacy

Because windows allow us to see out from inside the house, they also allow those on the outside to see in. Window treatments can provide the privacy you desire. Because we use different rooms for different purposes, they each have different privacy requirements. Public rooms, like living rooms, dens and kitchens, don't require as much privacy as bedrooms, bathrooms and other more personal rooms, where more privacy is desired.

Window treatments made of sheer and lightweight fabrics let light through, yet provide privacy during the daytime. Drapes or curtains made of heavier materials are needed behind these sheer materials at night when the interior lights are on.

Using window treatments often means you have to compromise some of the light your window lets in for some privacy—glass block and frosted or etched glass are window options that preserve your privacy and still bring lots of natural light into your home. Transom and clerestory windows are other windows that bring light into a room without sacrificing privacy.

Louvered blinds and shutters give you control of the amount of privacy and light that is let into a room.

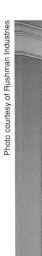

To demonstrate the true versatility of horizontal blinds, the louvers were adjusted on these Venetian blinds to create small windowlike openings just above the chairs. Horizontal blinds let in outside light without compromising privacy.

Cafe curtains on the lower half of this kitchen window provide privacy for those seated at the table, yet the top half is left open, allowing light to brighten the room.

A curtain rod and pleated shades are mounted below the top of the window to create the illusion of a smaller window with a transom above it. The curtains and shades are mounted at a height that ensures privacy for anyone using the room, leaving the top portion of the window open to let in light.

PLANNING

Design

The sizes and shapes of windows, and their composition in a window design, are the way windows bring personality to a room. You can direct light into a dark corner of a room or frame a favorite view with a well-planned window design. Tall windows, or windows positioned high on a wall like cathedral, clerestory and transom windows, shine light deep into rooms with high vaulted ceilings and help illuminate the large, spacious areas.

The colors and textures used in window treatments also greatly influence the appearance of a room. Light colors make the room seem larger, while dark colors are more intimate and make a space seem smaller. Smooth textures reflect light and make colors appear lighter and more lustrous. When a material has more texture, it appears duller, because the texture absorbs, rather than reflects, light. Window treatments with noticeable texture are usually more casual. Color and texture should balance one another. If a room has lots of color, down play the use of textures. If there's a lot of texture in the window treatment design, the color should be kept to a minimum to prevent the room from feeling too busy.

A fixed triangle window, an awning window and a curved-top transom window are combined to create a fun-shaped, fairy-tale window design for a child's room. This clever combination looks good both inside and outside.

Lofty cathedral-style windows are angled to follow the lines of the roof and highlight the handsome hardwood ceilings. This stunning group of windows creates a majestic frame for an incredible mountain view.

A portion of this room was built into a sloping hill, so well-placed, horizontal windows were used to effectively bring bright natural light to this ground-level eating area.

Photos top and left: courtesy of Crestline Windows

Photo courtesy of Spring Window Fashions

Ancient Greece was the inspiration for this bathroom. A round-top window is framed by a mural that depicts ancient Grecian pillars.

Pink, accordion-pleated shades create a subtle striped pattern when backlit with sunlight. The striped pattern is reflected in the fabric of one of the chairs in the room. In contrast to the soft, subtle stripes, paisley fabric was used to cover the cornice above the window and the other chair.

Clever use of window treatments can alter the apparent size and proportions of windows. Blinds, shades, curtains, drapes and top treatments can be mounted on windows in ways that alter the perceived dimensions of the window.

When blinds are mounted on the inside of a window, they reflect the actual size of the window. When mounted on the outside of the window, a shade or a blind will make the window seem wider than it actually is.

The placement of fabric treatments like curtains and drapes can also alter the perceived size of a window. When curtains are tied back high, the window appears narrower; low tiebacks create the sense of a wider window. Mounting curtains above the top of the window makes the window seem taller than it is; mounting them below the top can create the visual image of two smaller windows, or a window with a transom above it.

(above) Rich, red crushed velvet fabric creates a plush window treatment for this French door and window combination. The elegant top treatment features a combination of swags over a gathered valance with a satiny balloon valance just above the doors.

Photo courtesy of Kolbe & Kolbe Millwork Co.

The soothing lavender color of these designer shades brings serenity to this bedroom setting. The drape of the swags over the designer poles is reflected in the shape of the butterfly shades, which fan out when a string is pulled. They lie flat when lowered.

Photo courtesy of Cy DeCosse Inc.

Simple swags and drapes add an elegant, flowing touch to an ordinary window setting. The sheer lightweight material creates a classic look that's also bright and breezy.

Photo courtesy of Hurd Millwork Company

Opposite page bottom photo courtesy of Spring Window Fashions

The use of window treatments was kept to a minimum in order to fully enjoy the view in this antique-style alcove created by a double-sized bay window. Individual swags mounted over each window are a design detail that adds the finishing touch to this sunny retreat.

PLANNING

Light

Photo courtesy of Crestline Windows

The orientation, placement, size, shape and number of windows determine the way light enters and affects a room. Windows facing south and east let in warm, cheerful light. Northern light is softer and cooler, and light from the west is the strongest and most intense.

Light that comes in through high clerestory windows bounces off ceilings and walls, changing a room's character throughout the day. Cathedral windows emphasize the sweep of a raised ceiling and high roofline. Light through stained glass, leaded, beveled or etched glass can create dynamic accents and turn a window into a work of art.

You can direct the way light enters a room by designing a custom window combination. A well-chosen grouping of windows, positioned either vertically or side by side, can create a dazzling and functional window display that enhances the visual appeal of the house both inside and out.

Two casement windows come together to form a corner window. The light from both directions brightens the kitchen and keeps natural light in the kitchen as the sun moves across the sky during the day.

Photo courtesy of Loewen Windows

Impressive window groupings have a dramatic impact on this home both inside and out. Round-top windows create visual continuity and unify its architectural design.

A spacious room extension creates a bright poolside viewing platform. Light streams in through a glass roof that peaks at the roofline of the house. Floor-to-ceiling triple-hung windows, with attached muntins, flood the room with light and create a classic-looking bow window design.

A pop-out greenhouse unit is a sunny spot in this kitchen. Like a bow or a bay window, this greenhouse unit visually expands the room. Lush plants sit on the ledge, enjoying the extra room. The top of the unit is also glass, which creates even more open space than a simple bay window. Since the main reason for adding a greenhouse unit is to let in the sun, there is usually no need for window treatments.

To enjoy the maximum amount of light through a window, use a window treatment that clears the entire window when open. Sheer window treatments diffuse light and lessen the effects of the hot sun. Lining a window treatment also protects furniture and fabrics from sun damage.

Glass block, frosted, leaded and stained glass are specialty glasses that can be used in windows to effectively bring natural sunlight into a room without compromising any privacy.

Glass block is perfect for rooms like bathrooms that require a great deal of privacy, but generally don't have the wall space to accommodate high windows or skylights. A glass block wall will softly bathe a room with diffused light and still maintain an acceptable degree of privacy.

Light through beveled, leaded or stained glass is ever changing. These types of windows add style and intrigue as they playfully cast shadows, colors and patterns around a room.

Photo courtesy of Phifer Wire Products

Transparent screen shades and a glass block wall diffuse incoming light and create a soft backdrop for the contemporary industrial design of this urban loft. Even though they block the direct sun quite effectively, the sheer screens remain neutral in their visual impact on this room. Banks of recessed transom windows bounce light deep into the room.

Photo courtesy of ADO Corporation

Crisp white cotton curtains are gathered with blue bows to flood this kitchen with natural sunlight. Sheer curtains with the same delicate pastel print billow out from behind the formal curtains. The windows seem to glow softly when the sunlight comes through the sheers.

Photo courtesy of Devenco Products

The simple artistic design of the window is beautifully accentuated with horizontal blinds. There are as many different looks to be created as there are options for controlling the blinds.

Multiwindow combinations adorn the tall walls and bring the feel of the desert into this southwestern abode. By eliminating the interior walls and filling the exterior walls with windows, the link with the outdoors can be enjoyed from every room.

PLANNING

Bringing the Outdoors Inside

Windows, especially large ones, can expand the feeling of an interior space. They bring the outdoors inside by replacing a solid wall with transparent glass, allowing us to become a part of the outdoors while still inside. The world outside the window becomes a visual extension of the room.

French or patio doors can be opened to bring the color and fragrance of the outdoors inside and expand the living space of the room.

Minimal use of window treatments keeps the visual link between the inside and outside strong. Simple window treatments, like blinds, will keep the focus on what is outside the window, not on the window treatment.

Photo courtesy of Loewen Windows

(right) A picture window in a living room is combined with a casement window on either side and a large transom window above to create an impressive window wall. The decorative muntins add a traditional touch and accent the unique shape of the top window.

(below) Pool users enjoy the best of both worlds by this indoor pool. Warm, bright sunlight enters through sliding patio doors on all walls and a panel of skylights above. In bad weather, the outdoors can be closed off and the pool can still be enjoyed.

Photo courtesy of Hurd Millwork Company

Photo courtesy of Marvin Windows

A unique corner window gives this portion of the room the feel of a sunroom. Tall fixed windows are topped with transom windows to create a floor-to-ceiling wall of windows. The smaller vertical window is topped by an awning window that can be opened to let cool breezes blow through.

Photo courtesy of Crestline Windows

A cozy corner whirlpool enjoys light from two angles through large casement windows on adjoining walls. The casements can be cranked open to let you commune with nature, if desired.

A sunny piano room is enclosed by classic double-hung windows. The white muntins on the windows and small transoms give the room a traditional touch.

This sunny window combination includes casement windows and two quarter-circle, round-top windows. This clever combination brightens the bedroom, opens the corner and gives it character.

SELECTING WINDOWS

Windows open your home to the rest of the world. They enhance the design of your home with graceful shapes and openings. A carefully planned window design can put a beautiful frame around a favorite view and transform it into the focal point of a room.

Despite the variety in styles, windows can be classified in general by the way they function. Double-hung windows have two sashes that move up and down along grooves in the frame. Casement windows are hinged on the sides and open like doors with a crank or a push. Sliding windows are basically like double-hung windows mounted sideways. Awning windows are hinged at the top and open outward from the bottom, while hopper windows are just the opposite—hinged at the bottom, opening outward from the top. Fixed windows are mounted permanently in their frame and cannot be opened; these types of windows range from large picture windows to tiny accent windows.

With some window styles, you have the option of choosing what type of window is utilized. Bay windows can come with double-hung, casement or fixed windows—or a combination of window types. When combining several windows to create a complex window configuration, it is best to include operable windows along with stationary types.

A well-choreographed window plan creates a separate framed setting for each room of the house, yet utilizes common design elements like round-top transoms and vertically paneled skylights throughout to give continuity to the design of the house.

A large bow window and a French patio door bring warm sunlight into this roomy log cabin home. Two triangle-shaped transom windows, one above the French door and one above the bow window, keep the architectural design symmetrical and help illuminate the large vaulted ceiling.

A small round-top window brings just the right touch of style to this simple bedroom window. The arch of the window emphasizes the unique shape of the ceiling and bounces light deeper into the room.

A custom-designed transom montage joins a French patio door to fill the room with flair. Rounded transom windows above the door create an appealing entryway.

SELECTING WINDOWS

Buying Guide

Windows are composed of different types of glass; two of the most common are flat glass or ordinary window glass, and insulating glass, made of two or more panes sealed together with space between the panes to trap air. The climate you live in and the type of insulation your home needs will be the most important factors in determining what kind of glass your windows should have.

Windows are also rated for energy efficiency by R-values and U-values. R-values indicate the energy efficiency of the window unit.

The U-value is the rate of heat flow through the window.

Even though the traditional wood frame is still commonly used, manufacturers are also making windows with aluminum- and vinyl-clad frames that don't need painting or maintenance. Some wood-frame windows are also available with a polymer coating in a variety of colors, and don't need painting.

Check the thickness of your walls, before ordering patio doors and windows, by measuring the jamb on an existing door or window.

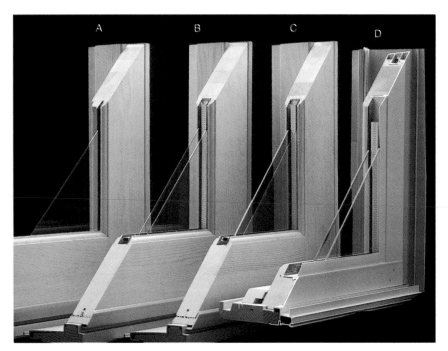

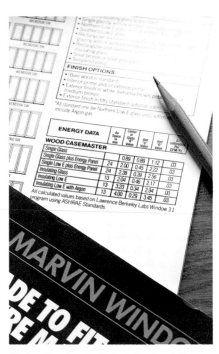

Single-pane glass (A) is suitable only in very mild climates. Double-pane windows (B) have a sealed air space between the layers of glass to reduce heat loss. They are available with different insulating abilities, some have "low E" glass which has an invisible coating of metal on one surface, and some are filled with an inert gas, like argon. Double-glazed tinted glass (C) reduces heat buildup. Tempered glass (D) is used for patio doors and large picture windows because of its extra strength.

Higher R-values indicate better insulating properties. Top-quality windows can have an R-value as high as 4.0. The lower the U-value, the more energy efficient the window. A window with a U-value of 0.2 or 0.3 is considered very good. The colder the climate, the more important the low U-value.

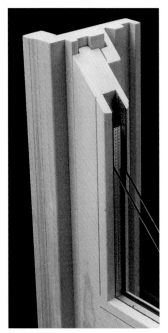
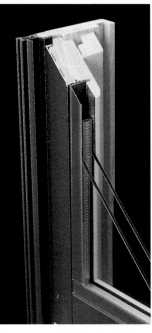
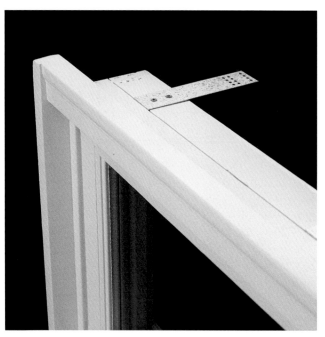

Wood frames (left) are still popular. They are a good choice for windows and patio doors used in remodeling projects, because their preattached exterior brick molding blends well with the look of existing windows. Clad-frame windows (right) feature an aluminum or vinyl shell, so they don't need painting. They are used most frequently in new construction and are attached with nailing flanges that fit underneath the siding material.

Polymer coatings are optional on some wood-frame windows. Polymer-coated windows and doors are available in a variety of colors, and do not need painting.

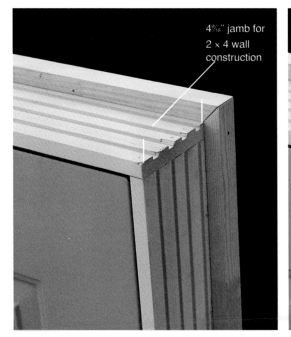
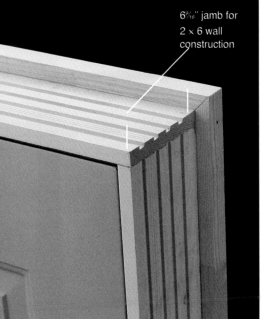

Manufacturers offer literally thousands of variations of window styles and designs in stock sizes with an array of framing and glazing options. If the window you want isn't offered in a standard size, many manufacturers will customize the frame jambs to match whatever wall construction you have. Find your wall thickness by measuring the jamb width on an existing door or window.

WINDOW STYLES

Traditional Views

Casement, double-hung, sliding, fixed and awning windows are traditional window styles that have proven their value and necessity throughout the years. Casement windows have a contemporary look. They pivot on hinges mounted on the sides, and crank or push open, providing good ventilation and an unobstructed view out the window. Casements also work well as egress windows.

Double-hung windows slide up and down and have a traditional look. Instead of the troublesome sash weights found on older double-hung windows, modern double-hung windows have a spring-mounted operating mechanism.

Sliding windows are basically double-hung windows turned sideways. Sliding windows are inexpensive and require little maintenance, but they don't provide as much open ventilation as casement windows because only half of the window can be open at one time.

Fixed windows include any window that is mounted permanently in its frame and cannot be opened. From expansive picture windows to tiny accents and transoms, fixed windows come in many standard shapes, including rectangular, triangular, trapezoidal, semicircular and elliptical. If you can't find the fixed window you desire in a standard size, you can usually custom-order the exact shape and size you need from a manufacturer.

Awning windows are hinged at the top and open outward from the bottom. They work well in combination with fixed windows because they fit easily above or below other types of windows and are able to provide ventilation without letting in rain. This makes them a good choice in damp climates.

Photo courtesy of Wenco Windows

These three individual double-hung windows are part of a bay window that brings badly needed light to this dark room. Each window opens and closes separately so outside breezes are easily controlled.

Photo courtesy of Loewen Windows

Three fixed transom windows sit neatly on top of a set of tall casement windows, letting in light that brightens this bathroom. Thin muntins and mullions tie the group together and enhance its traditional charm.

Photo courtesy of Marvin Windows

As part of a cathedral window design, these classic casement windows are an intrinsic part of the larger window display. Sliding windows are available in larger sizes than their double-hung cousins, because they don't require the weight mechanisms of double-hung windows. They're also easier to operate.

Photo courtesy of Eagle Window Designs

A hopper window functions like an awning window, except, with a hopper window, the bottom is hinged and the top swings in to open. Because hopper windows allow most of the air to pass over the top, they help control the comfort in a room by diverting chilly breezes and stimulating air circulation throughout the room.

31

WINDOW STYLES

Broaden Your Horizons with Bays & Bows

Many elegant and interesting window styles can be purchased ready-made, in a range of styles and sizes. Bay and bow windows are examples of specialty windows that are available in almost any size. Bay windows extend out from a structure with one or more straight center windows and two angled side windows. Bow windows also extend out from a structure, but the windows, which can vary in number, form a smooth outward curve.

Because they extend outward from the wall, these windows expand the sense of space in a room and make it feel larger without expensive structural changes. Available in a number of sizes and styles, they can include fixed or operable windows, or a combination of both.

Photo courtesy of Eagle Window Designs

Photo courtesy of Marvin Windows

Two casement windows that open to allow ventilation are a part of the design that makes this bow window efficient, as well as elegant. The smooth line of the curve distinguishes a bow from a bay window.

Two casement windows are joined with a fixed window to create one large bay window. Decorative grilles have been attached to create a consistent overall look. Some bays extend all the way to the floor, while others, like this one, include a built-in window seat that makes the additional space more usable.

An arched cathedral window brings light high into the rafters of this formal study, brightening the dark room and warming the rich tones of the wood.

WINDOW STYLES

High Lights for your Home

Clerestory (pronounced *clear-story*), cathedral and transom windows are positioned high on a wall to bring extra light deep into a room for a more dramatic effect. Clerestory windows are found on walls that rise above the roof or other parts of the building. Also called ribbon windows, clerestory windows are positioned high along the roofline, admitting light into central interior areas without sacrificing privacy.

Cathedral windows often span the height of two levels. They emphasize the sweep of a raised ceiling and high roofline, flooding a space with light. In homes where cathedral windows are used, rooms on the upper floors often have openings facing them so they can share the light and view.

Skylights bring sunlight into rooms that have limited wall space for windows. Round-top and transom windows work best in tandem with other larger windows. They bring style and design to ordinary window configurations to create striking visual images. Transom windows are often used as accents for French and patio doors. Round-top windows can usually be found in combination with a large picture window or patio door. A round-top window can change the entire look and feel of a room, both inside and out. Palladian windows are a type of round-top window with a design that includes an arch within an arch, and muntins that connect the two arches creating a a sunburst design.

These windows transform the way light and shadow play on walls and floors, changing a room's character throughout the day. They can be arranged in infinite combinations and patterns; and with careful planning, you can add a sunny accent anywhere you want.

A group of skylights are incorporated as an element of design that takes advantage of the unique shape of the roof. These windows give visual interest to a large, angled ceiling, while directing lots of natural light into the space.

An elegant arrangement of casement and cathedral windows opens an entire wall of the room to the deck and the view of the lake just outside. Cathedral windows, high on one wall, bounce light off the high ceiling and around this spacious room.

35

WINDOW STYLES

Patio & French Doors—Gateways to the Great Outdoors

French doors and sliding patio doors extend your living space by providing a link between the indoors and outdoors. These doors work like windows the way they bring light, view and ventilation into a room. When they are open, the room actually expands into the outdoor space.

A sliding door consists of two-door panels of tempered glass in a wood, vinyl or aluminum frame. Sliding patio doors offer good visibility and lighting. Because they slide on tracks and require no floor space for operation, sliding doors are a good choice for cramped spaces where swinging doors won't fit.

A French door is a pair of hinged doors with one inactive door held stationary by slide bolts at the top and bottom, and an active door closing and locking against it. French patio doors bring a classic elegance to a room. Weathertight models are used to join indoor and outdoor living areas, while indoor models are used to link two rooms. Because they open on hinges, your room design must allow space for the doors to swing.

A poolside cabana gets a beautiful framed view of the scene outside through a set of three French doors. With all of the French doors opened, the room feels as if it has no walls. The large wooden louvered shutters, attached to each of the French doors, can be closed for privacy.

The white muntins on the transom, the sidelights and the door itself give this sliding patio door the look of a traditional French door. The large glass door and windows, with decorative snap-on grilles, create a delicate division between the room and the great outdoors. Those inside can enjoy an uninterrupted view from the comfort of the indoors.

Selecting Window Treatments

Window treatments do more than just dress your windows, they filter and direct light during the day and keep the darkness out at night. They also provide privacy and insulation from the elements outside. Window treatments are an integral part of a room's decorating scheme. They can be a part of a room's interior design motif, or the focal point of the room.

Window treatments can be used to emphasize architectural details or add visual width and height to a window. While some window treatments are the centerpiece of a room, others are a subtle backdrop for other elements in the room.

From breezy, open-weave curtains and blinds, to thick, elegant draperies and fancy top treatments, the possibilities for creative and functional window treatments are almost endless.

These delicate lace curtain panels can be used alone or as an undertreatment. The lace pattern diffuses light and fills the room with soft shadows.

Light, flowing fabric is draped softly over a decorator curtain rod above two facing corner windows. The simple white window treatment frames this setting and creates a cozy niche for reading and relaxing.

Even the windows are dressed for dinner in this formal setting. Long flowing curtains and ornate cornices give this dining room traditional style and elegance.

Louvered wooden shutters control the amount of light that comes into a room in two ways: first, they open and close like a set of double doors for complete sunlight or complete privacy; second, the louvers can be adjusted to varying degrees of light.

Designer hardware adds pizzazz to this simple pleated shade. The soft texture and drape of the material echo the look and feel of the material in the sofa.

SELECTING WINDOW TREATMENTS

Buying Guide

Window treatments, like draperies and curtains, need hardware to be mounted properly. Hardware for window treatments can be decorative, to enhance the beauty of the treatment, or strictly conventional, made primarily for function and designed to be concealed behind the window treatment. Many stores offer a variety of decorative window treatment accessories, such as curtain rings, finials (decorative attachments for the ends of curtain rods), ornamental brackets, swag holders and tieback holders, along with standard window treatment hardware. These items are available in various materials, including solid brass, brass plate, copper, wrought iron and wood, as well as plastic.

Depending on the visual effect you want, you can mount an outside treatment that covers just the window frame, or extend it beyond the frame onto the walls. Mounting curtains above the top of the window makes the window appear

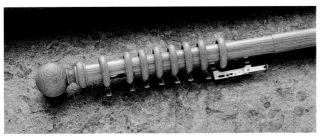

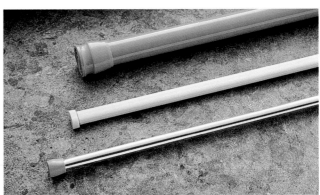

Wood poles, hand drawn (bottom), or traverse (top), come in various lengths, diameters, and finishes. The pole and any decorative brackets, inside-mount sockets, rings, or elbow returns are purchased separately.

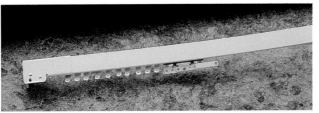

All of the traverse rods and pole sets shown above come in a variety of styles and materials to match any room decor from traditional to contemporary. Conventional traverse rods (top) are available in white, ivory and wood tones. Flexible traverse rods (bottom), are for use on bay windows.

Sash rods (top), hold sash curtains snugly against French doors and windows. Tension rods (center) have a spring mechanism to hold the rod within the frame. Cafe rods (bottom) are used for hand-drawn window treatments.

taller. You can make the window seem wider by adjusting the width of the curtain rod in comparison to the window.

There are two basic kinds of curtain rods: stationary rods for hand-drawn or fixed curtains and traverse rods for mechanically drawn drapes. Adjustable traverse rods are used for draperies that open and close with a cord. Two-way traverse rods work by moving the panels from the center to the ends and back. These rods are some of the most popular drapery hardware used today. One-way traverse rods move only one panel in one direction and are used most often over sliding patio doors. Stationary rods slide through traditional rod-pocket curtains and valances and adjust to various widths.

Decorative types of stationary rods range from simple round rods to fluted types with ornate details. Concealed rods are single flat rods made with projections ranging from 1¼ to 4 inches in order to clear other treatments beneath them. Sash rods and tension rods are other common types of concealed rods.

Specialty rods include flat rods that are hinged to fit corner and bay windows, and custom-bent and flexible rods that follow curves on arched windows. Combination rods allow you to hang several treatments on one piece of hardware.

To mount blinds or shades on the inside of a window, measure the width within the frame at the top, center and bottom. For the height, measure within the frame from the top to the sill. Allow ½" clearance between the bottom of the drapery and the floor when measuring for floor-length draperies. For loosely woven fabrics, allow 1" clearance.

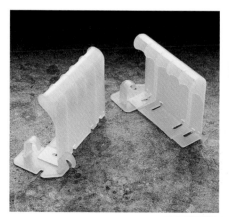

Other hardware accessories include concealed and decorative tieback holders and swag holders. Concealed tieback holders (left) are designed to fit discreetly behind a drapery or curtain. Decorative tieback holders (center) are prominently displayed as part of the design of the window treatment. Decorative tieback holders can also be used like swag holders (right) to support the fabric in a swag curtain.

WINDOW TREATMENTS
Curtains & Draperies

Window treatments have expanded beyond the established and predictable pleated panels of yesterday, to include exciting new fabrics, hardware and headings in imaginative combinations. Draperies, considered more formal that curtains, are generally made of richer, heavier fabrics. Sheers, made from lightweight opaque drapery fabric, are often used as a soft undertreatment for draperies. Curtains are normally smaller, lighter and more casual than draperies, so curtain rods are smaller than drapery rods. Curtains are either gathered on a rod or attached to a rod by tabs, rings or ties.

A rod pocket is the most common way of hanging a curtain. The curtain has a stitched pocket or casing at the top, through which a rod is threaded. Many seemingly elaborate gathered curtains are just variations on the basic rod-pocket curtain. Tab curtains have tabs sewn to the top of each curtain panel, to slip easily over a decorative rod, creating gentle folds. Tiebacks not only hold curtain panels in place, they are a popular way to add a finishing touch to a window treatment. They can be used to add color, texture, and interest to otherwise ordinary draperies.

Different fabrics can dramatically change the effect a window treatment has on a room. Mediumweight and heavyweight fabrics give the room a formal feel. They provide good insulation, light control and privacy, especially at night. Sheer curtains filter light and provide privacy in the daytime, but to maintain this privacy they need heavier curtains behind them at night. Linings increase the life of curtains, reduce noise, block light and add insulation. Lined curtains have more body and hang better than unlined ones.

Length is another variable with draperies and curtains. To ensure that all draperies in a room are the same height from the floor, use the highest window in the room as the standard for measuring for the treatments on the other windows. Full-length curtains work in both elegant and informal settings. Short curtains that cover the lower half of the window are called cafe curtains. They let light in and still preserve privacy.

Heavy satin fabric and brass hardware make these draperies elegant and sleek. The top treatments are tailor-made to maintain the streamlined look of the draperies. Lace curtains soften the look and diffuse the light as it comes through the windows.

A triple set of curtains uses color and fabric to create and emphasize depth in this elegant window treatment. The long draperies flow into folded pools on each side of the window. The lower edges are delicately held back, as if taking a bow for this dramatic design.

This simple curtain with ruffled trim and tiebacks is a country classic. The curtain, made of light-weight fabric in a neutral color, creates a pleasant contrast to the busy wallpaper pattern.

Photo courtesy of Conrad Imports. Design: Barbara Mack/Fleece to Fibers. Photo: Jame Boa Photography

An open-weave shade complements the jungle motif of this window setting. The sheer shade lets you enjoy the view with some privacy and the texture goes well with the animal print design on the chair cover and the trim on the draperies.

WINDOW TREATMENTS

Blinds, Shutters & Shades

Combining window treatments like curtains, draperies, and top treatments with a complementary blind or shade is a popular way to create a fresh new look for a window.

Blinds come in horizontal and vertical styles; both have slats that compactly stack up and tilt for privacy and light control. They come in an array of colors and sizes and materials including wood, plastic and metal. Blinds can be used to reflect sunlight away from the windows in the summer and let it in during the winter.

Shades are as versatile in use as they are in style. They provide privacy, block light and conserve energy. Popular shade styles include Austrian shades, which draw up into scalloped folds, and

Roman shades, which form neat horizontal folds. Balloon shades form billows, and cloud shades create soft, cloudlike poufs.

Wooden shutters have long been a popular window treatment, adding charm to any window setting. Accordion-fold shutters can be used on almost any window: they close for privacy and open neatly to expose the full width of a window. Shutters with louvers offer greater light control than many window treatments. The louvers allow you to control the amount and direction of light. They also provide privacy, ventilation and insulation, much like a blind. Shutters can be painted or stained to match the window frame.

When the pleated pastel shades are closed and sunlight shines from behind, this patio door and round-top window become a work of art. When open, these shades create an entirely different atmosphere for the room. A matching pleated shade in a smaller window nearby maintains the design.

The traditional look of wooden louvered shutters is a well-chosen window treatment for this formal dining room. The louvers and the accordion-fold design let a pleasant amount of light in without being obtrusive.

Accordion-style wooden shutters unfold to let in as much light as desired. Wooden shutters can be painted to match any color in the room, or they can be stained and finished to match any woodwork.

Traditional Venetian blinds work quite well as a window treatment for this bay window with a view. The louvers keep the sunlight under control and the blinds don't distract from the look of the window or its view.

WINDOW TREATMENTS

Top Treatments

Top treatments can be used with other window treatments, like draperies and shades, or they can be used alone as a subtle accent. The styles of top treatments range from softly gathered or pleated valances, to rigid boxlike cornices, with an assortment of styles in between.

Valances are shortened versions of curtains, draperies and shades. Gathered valances are the most popular of all top treatments. Available in a number of styles, they can be formal or casual, depending on their shape and fabric. Box-pleated, balloon, cloud, Austrian and pouf valances are all shortened forms of the shades.

Swags are among the easiest and most impressive top treatments you can use. They add a soft, flowing, classic look to a window. To make a basic swag, drape the fabric over a decorative rod or hardware, and arrange as desired. The key to beautiful swags is draping and arranging them.

A cornice is a box-type frame that is used as a top treatment. A cornice not only frames and finishes a window treatment, it also hides unsightly hardware. Cornices can be covered with wallpaper or lightly padded and covered with fabric. Smaller, thin cornices have a sleek look and are especially suitable for contemporary rooms.

The length of a top treatment should be in proportion to the total length of the window treatment. For valances, this length is usually about one-fifth of the window treatment, but cornices may be shorter to prevent them from appearing too overpowering or top-heavy.

Kolbe & Kolbe Millwork Co.

A sheer swag divides this window into two sections. The round-top portion of the window acts like a transom window.

Photo courtesy of Spring Window Fashions

(right) The old-fashioned look of the lace bishop sleeve curtain emphasizes the classic beauty of the leaded glass in the window.

A large sculpted cornice neatly balances the rich plush look of the gathered draperies. A sheer Austrian shade adds texture and interest for a complete look.

Custom draperies are topped by a beautifully styled three-swag combination. The decorative hardware and dramatic detail in the top treatment create an art deco design.

A PORTFOLIO

of Window
& Window Treatment Ideas

DELIGHTFUL DOUBLE-HUNGS

Double-hung windows are still the most common window style found in traditional houses today. They have two sashes that slide along grooves in the frame; an upper, or outside, sash that moves down, and a lower, or inside, sash that moves up. The sash movements and positions are controlled by springs, weights or friction devices. Some double-hungs are really single-hung, meaning that only the bottom sash moves.

The number of options for window treatments that will work in double-hung windows is almost unlimited. Anything goes, as long as it doesn't interfere with the operation of the window.

Photo courtesy of Marvin Windows

A solid row of double-hung windows on two adjoining walls of this house become the base for a pyramid of windows in a corner. Decorative moldings and window trim reflect the traditional feel of the classic architecture in the home.

A sunny bay, composed of three triple-hung windows, bounces soft sunlight into a narrow room. The balloon shades mounted above each window are pulled up to create softly gathered shapes. When lowered, the shades lie flat and have a decorative scalloped bottom edge.

The classic look of the white-clad double-hung windows is reinforced by the simple swags draped over each window. Decorative brass swag holders add a nice finishing touch to this unique round room.

(left) Dress up a double-hung window by draping it with a tieback curtain and topping it with a decorative cornice. With a thoughtful window treatment, an ordinary window becomes the focal point of a room's decor.

(below) The heavy weight and texture of the curtains calls for heavier-looking hardware. Thick brass poles hold the narrow curtains up. Decorative tieback holders keep curtains in place. Since the curtains are purely decorative and cannot be closed completely for privacy, a matching pleated shade dresses the window as well.

Cafe curtains cover the bottom half of this casement window, letting the warm sunlight in through the top half. A decorative border frames the window and eliminates the need for any other window treatment. The rustic wood paneling, window frame and muntins create the perfect frame for the view of the wilderness just outside.

This large bump-out addition is created by a combination of tall casement windows in a bow window setting. The immense size of this bow creates an entire addition to the room, not just an expanded corner. Round-top windows emphasize the domed ceiling and bounce light high into the ceilings, accenting the rounded architecture.

CLASSIC CASEMENTS

Casement windows are hinged on the side and swing outward. Hung singly or in pairs, they provide excellent ventilation because the window can be opened completely, allowing the outward sash to catch the breeze and guide it into the house.

Casement windows can make a dramatic statement when combined with other windows and window styles like round-top, bow or bay windows. They are available in a number of sizes and in both right-hand and left-hand models. The swing direction must be specified when ordering.

Shades and blinds, with or without a valance, work well on casements, as do most other window treatments. The important thing to remember when dressing a casement window is to make sure the window treatment doesn't interfere with the crank mechanism.

Photos courtesy of Marvin Windows

The bay window in this kitchen incorporates five classic-style casement windows. Each window can be individually cranked open as much or as little as desired. Any use of window treatments would be too much for this bright, crisp setting, with its busy wallpaper pattern and floral border. The decorative muntins are enough to give the windows a finished look.

57

A handsome combination of casement windows with a decorative arched top lets light into the nooks and crannies of this room. A simple lace curtain is mounted across the lower portion of the window to bring some privacy to the bedroom. The elegant line of the top of the window has been left exposed to emphasize the arched ceiling above it.

Two double casement windows on adjoining walls meet to form a sunny reading corner. Lightweight curtains are draped over decorative poles to form soft swags and bishops sleeves curtains. Off-white pleated shades diffuse the sunlight yet keep the corner bright and cheery.

A distinctive cornice is produced by covering vent hoses with fabric. These decorative cornices are mounted by inserting curtain rods into each of the vent hoses. A simple pleated shade can be raised or lowered to let in as much of the outside as desired.

Fixed and casement windows comprise this stately window combination. A row of tall fixed windows sits atop a row of smaller windows, two of which are casements that can be opened to circulate fresh air through this lofty mountain retreat.

Floor-to-ceiling casement windows topped by transoms provide the view that is the backdrop for this formal dining room. The sleek, tailored style of the drapes and top treatment help create an elegant atmosphere in the room.

The sliding window in the center of this window group is topped with a fixed round-top window. The snap-on grilles are optional but have been added to repeat a design element used on other windows in the house.

SENSIBLE SLIDERS

Sliding windows are basically double-hung windows turned sideways. The sashes slide horizontally along tracks in the frame. In double-sliding windows, both sashes move; in single-sliding windows, one sash is fixed.

Sliding windows give about the same ventilation and air circulation as double-hung windows, but they aren't as tricky to operate because they don't need weights or balancing mechanisms. Sliding windows are available in larger sizes than double-hung windows because they're easier to operate.

This streamlined sliding window goes well with the sleek contemporary design of the kitchen. No window treatments are necessary.

(right) This simple sliding window frames a lovely view and creates a cozy backdrop for the dining area. The draped swag top treatment and the snap-in muntins add an old-fashioned charm.

(below) Pleated shades and custom-designed cornices dress the sliding windows in this luxury bathroom. The two smaller sliding windows that form the corner behind the whirlpool can be easily opened from within the tub.

ALLURING AWNING WINDOWS

Awning windows are hinged at the top and open outward from the bottom. They are great companions to larger fixed windows because they go together gracefully with many different window styles. When combined with other windows in a group, awning windows provide an easy way to create ventilation where a fixed window alone would offer none.

Photo courtesy of Loewen Windows

Photo courtesy of Loewen Windows

(above, left) A large awning window above a kitchen sink pops open easily for quick ventilation.

(above, right) Placed between two decoratively shaped fixed windows, the awning window can be pushed open to let fresh air in. This delightful window design brings something special to a child's bedroom.

Photo courtesy of SNE Enterprises Inc.

Large window areas like this one bring in lots of light; they also bring in heat as well. Awning windows along the bottom of the group were a wise choice: they can be opened to allow air to circulate and cool the room.

Awning windows are incorporated into this large window grouping to help get fresh air circulating throughout this large open space. The awning windows are located around the living room area at the perfect height to bring a cool breeze to anyone lounging on the sofa.

This convenient awning window was included in this grouping because it can be opened to let in fresh air. Since awning windows swing open from the bottom, they prevent rain from coming in, so they can be opened any time, even when it's raining.

BEAUTIFUL BAY WINDOWS

Although a bay window is treated as a single unit, it is actually a group of windows, with side windows that are angled and a middle window or windows that are parallel to the wall. Some bay windows have window seats, while others open to the floor.

Bay windows give a historic, old-fashioned, look to a structure and add an interesting flair to the architecture. They expand the living space in a room and bring in more light and more of the outside view than traditional casement or double-hung windows.

Photo courtesy of Marvin Windows

This bay window is a distinct design element in the detailed architecture of this home. The shape of the window dictates the shape of the entire structure. The result is a tower that has the look of an old-time New England lighthouse.

Photo courtesy of SNE Enterprises, Inc.

Photo courtesy of Marvin Windows

Bay windows not only add space and charm to the inside of a home, they also add traditional character to the outside of a house.

This sunny bay window expands the living area and fills the room with light. A small window seat in the bay is an ideal spot to place plants and flowers. The two side windows of this bay are operable casement windows that allow refreshing breezes to enter from either direction.

A simple bay window adds old-fashioned charm to any room. This cozy bay includes a roomy window seat with a breathtaking view just outside. When the window seat is not in use, it becomes a showcase for decorative vases and dried flower arrangements.

A 45% angled bay composed of three tall casement windows creates a small triangle-shaped window seat. This uniquely shaped pop-out lets in plenty of light and dramatically expands the sense of space in the room. It also becomes a distinct design element on the outside of the house.

Cafe curtains and plain gathered valances are hung with ordinary tension rods in this bay window. The window seat provided by this bay is a convenient shelf for this quaint breakfast niche.

Woodgrain accordion-fold shutters are used on this floor-to-ceiling bay window. The casual look of the wooden shutters combines with the wicker furniture to create an almost tropical motif for the room. The shutters can be completely opened to enjoy the full effect of the window or the louvers can be used to control the amount of light desired.

Flexible tension rods mount fancy balloon shades into this bay window. The rich material gives the shades a crepelike texture when raised. When lowered, they provide a rich backdrop for the beautiful wood window seat.

BOUNTIFUL BOW WINDOWS

Bow windows are similar to bay windows, except the panes in a bow window curve to form a smooth arc instead of the sharp angles formed by a bay window. Bow windows are available in a number of standard sizes or they can be custom-built.

Photo courtesy of Crestline Windows

A magnificent dining room table slides gently into the niche created by this stunning bow window. The tall fixed windows and awning windows along the bottom are framed and painted to reflect the accent trim used around the vaulted ceiling.

Photo courtesy of Crestline Windows

Casement windows are combined to form a very subtle bow window. The amount of actual room expansion is minimal, but the feeling of expanded space is still evident. The bottom of the bow makes a great shelf for plants and current reading materials.

Flexible curtain rods are used to mount a decorator valance along a transom that separates the tall casement windows from the overhead transom windows in this bow configuration. Tieback curtains frame a sunny breakfast niche created by the expanded space provided by the bow window.

The heavy plush window treatments on this bow window serve to unify the entire room. Additional details like a balloon shade and fringed tieback holders also tie into the room's design and contribute to the overall look and richness that this window treatment brings.

RADIANT ROUND-TOP WINDOWS

Round-top windows, also known as circle-top or semicircle windows, can be combined with existing traditional windows to create a beautiful one-of-a-kind window design.

Round-top windows give a home a traditional touch and are a charming way to accent the classic arched doorways and curving lines in a home's architecture. In contemporary-style architecture they enhance the geometrical design and add an interesting flair.

Sunlight from a clerestory window streams across three perfectly positioned round-top windows. These stately round-tops showcase the house from the outside and add a stunning view to this grand living room.

A well-planned window design makes excellent use of round-top windows to showcase this impressive home. The unified look adds a traditional flair and emphasizes the classic style.

(above) A classically designed round-top window adds distinguished elegance to this grand staircase. The large window adds a dramatic element to an otherwise empty wall space.

(right) A large round-top window spans a glass entry door that is flanked by two large glass sidelights. Decorative muntins form a sunburst pattern that shows off the expansive window.

A billowing swag is pulled through swag holders at the top and sides of this round-top window and made into puffy rosettes. The cascades softly frame the window as they flow to the floor. The swooping line of the swag plays artfully against the pattern made by the muntins in the round-top.

A custom blind fans open in this round-top to create a stunning sunburst over casement windows with matching pleated shades. White molding ou and accents the shape of the window.

A special curved curtain rod is used to mount a dreamy cloud shade snugly into this round-top window.

(right) Swag holders fashioned as petite bows hold a dainty swag that dresses this round-top window.

(below) Three large round-top windows form this sunny bay sitting area. A lightweight swag is draped around a thick, curved decorative wooden pole. Loose knots and cascades flow down the walls to separate each window and bring warm earthy tones and soft texture to the space.

UNCOMMON CATHEDRAL WINDOWS

Cathedral windows add elegance and drama to rooms with high ceilings. They bring light to the first and second floors of a home and make a room seem larger. By replacing the solid wall with glass, cathedral windows open up the space and give a room the sense of expanding to the outside.

It is common not to use any window treatments on cathedral windows to let as much natural light and beauty in as possible. If a window treatment is used, it is usually positioned to cover the lower portion of the window only.

Once a source of heat loss, windows with large glass areas, like cathedral windows, now can be extremely energy efficient, because they are available with specially treated glass that works to keep a room cool in the summer and warm in the winter.

Photo courtesy of Crestline Windows

Rooms with high ceilings and tall walls are the perfect settings for a dazzling cathedral window display.

Photo courtesy of Hurd Millwork Company

Artistically placed muntins divide this cathedral window into smaller geometric shapes. The pointed peak of the windows follows the angled lines of the gabled wall and roofline. This splendid window brings an equally splendid view into this spacious setting.

Photo courtesy of Eagle Window Designs

Distinctively tall cathedral windows seem to shoot upward into the tall cathedral ceiling, which tapers in at the top to form recessed rounded alcoves for the arched windows.

Photo courtesy of Loewen Windows

A sensational window ensemble makes a grand room even grander. Thin muntins divide the expansive area of glass into smaller, more delicate, sections. A graceful swag is hung at average ceiling height to bring perspective to the social area.

(right) Deep green pleated shades fan out and create a dramatic contrast against the neutral colors of the walls, emphasizing the geometric design of the window display. A tubelike cornice is covered with the same upholstery fabric used elsewhere in the room.

(below) Understated sheer Roman shades gently control the light in this contemporary living room. Even when the shades are closed, they admit diffused light that gives the room a soft glow.

CREATIVE CLERESTORYS

A true clerestory window is one that is located on a wall that rises above, and overlooks, the roofs of lower parts of the structure. A broader definition of clerestory windows includes ribbon windows. Ribbon windows consist of a window placed near the ceiling, usually in an unusual, slanted shape that follows the roofline. A truly efficient and inexpensive detail to include in a room's window design, clerestory and ribbon windows raise the view and fill a room with light without sacrificing privacy. They are an effective way to bring natural overhead light to smaller rooms, like kitchens and bathrooms, that don't have the wall space for windows.

Photo courtesy of Architectural Components, Inc.

Clerestory windows are styled with decorative muntins to match other existing windows and preserve the historic look of the interior of this home. Located on the second story of the room, the clerestory windows bring in enough light to brighten the high ceiling.

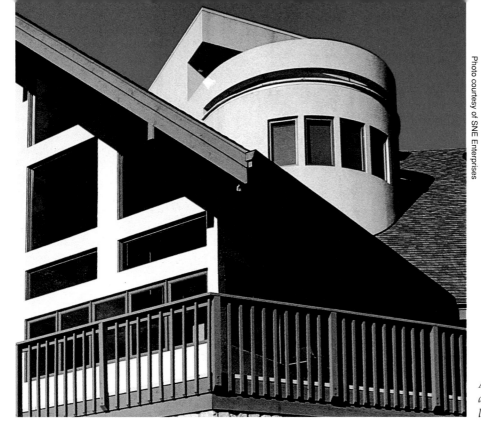

A line of small, square clerestory windows accent this unique turret and overlook the lower rooftops of this distinctive home.

Three round-top windows are punctuated by three ribbon windows directly above. The high windows flood the room with light and add a dramatic visual impact to a large, expansive wall.

Large clerestory windows are angled at the top to follow the graceful shape of this peaked gable wall. The magnificent window beautifully frames a majestic mountain view.

SENSATIONAL SIDELIGHTS & TRANSOMS

Sidelights and transom windows are often combined with exterior doors to create distinctive and dramatic entryways. Window manufacturers produce coordinating components that enable you to use sidelights and transoms in a variety of combinations with other windows and doors.

Transoms are usually operating windows that are included as part of a grouped window design that features large fixed windows. They not only add comfort control, they can also add a distinct accent to a window arrangement without compromising the integrity of the home's design.

Photo courtesy of Devenco Products

A transom in the shape of a half circle provides an interesting cutout shape that accents this entry door.

Photo courtesy of Spring Window Fashions

Solid sculpted cornices and a decorative beam divide small transom windows from the living room windows below. The decorative beam becomes a shelf that holds plants and highlights the windows and the upper portion of the room.

A narrow transom window is tucked above a small kitchen window. This tiny transom will let in lots of light and air, even when the wooden shutters mounted on the lower portion of the window are closed.

Custom-shaped ribbon windows are angled to follow the lines of this vaulted ceiling. A curtain rod placed at normal height brings a comfortable perspective to the living area.

Photo courtesy of Hurd Millwork Company

Snap-on grilles are an important detail; they unify the look of the transom, patio door and other windows with the style of this home.

Photo courtesy of Eagle Window Designs

Leaded and frosted glass are used in the sidelights and transom that surround this entry door. This decorative doorway makes every entrance a dramatic one.

SPECIALTY GLASS TREATMENTS

Decorative and specialty glass treatments, like beveled, etched, stained, or leaded glass, turn plain windows into works of art. The treated glass reflects light into a room, changing throughout the day. Stained or etched glass window treatments provide an element of privacy without blocking any incoming light.

Windows that feature specially treated glass are usually fixed, but they can be installed as movable units. Specialty glass is often delicate and subject to damage, so it is usually sealed between panes of ordinary glass to protect the window and simplify cleaning.

Photo courtesy of Stelz Studios

Photo courtesy of Eagle Window Designs

(above) A custom-designed stained glass window becomes an illuminated piece of three-dimensional art when light shines through from behind.

(right) Brass inlay and a feathery frosted design are delicate details that make this leaded glass window dramatic.

A group of three casement windows features a dazzling stained glass design. A transom window with an elegant curved top, also made of stained glass, unifies the combination.

The sleek lines of this French door create a sophisticated, open entrance. Glass block walls fill the space with light without compromising privacy.

Colorful spots of stained glass and creative use of leaded glass create an elegant art deco design. The frosted glass creates a solid background for the decorative window design.

Frosted and leaded glass makes a charming pattern that runs across this row of narrow transom windows. The design mimics the rippled edge of the roof.

SOARING SKYLIGHTS

Skylights are the perfect way to brighten rooms with soft overhead light without sacrificing privacy. They work especially well for getting light to small interior rooms and those that have limited wall space for windows. Skylights create openings in the ceiling overhead. They expand the feeling of space and add interest and detail to the room's design.

Skylights are available in stationary and venting styles. The effect these windows have on a room depends on their size and placement. They can be strategically positioned to bring a pocket of light into a specific part of a room that is hard to illuminate with natural light, or to cast sunlight and shadows throughout the room.

Opposite page, top photo courtesy of Andersen Windows.

Photo courtesy of Hurd Millwork Inc.

Overhead sunlight is pulled into this indoor pool area through skylights in the ceiling. The row of skylights joins the glass walls to create an atmosphere that gives pool users the benefits of being outdoors and the comfort of being indoors.

A large group of skylight windows bring warm light and add interesting design to an otherwise blank ceiling. A diamond-shaped window at the peak of the gable shines into the room like a star.

(left) Skylights line the roof and a multitude of windows expand the space in this contemporary studio. The ultramodern style is enhanced by the visual images created by the dramatic window design.

(right) A matching pleated shade latches to cover this skylight window. Sunlight still filters through the pleated shade and fills the room with soft, natural light.

Wood-framed French doors invite the outdoors into this sunny atrium. Transom and sidelight windows combine with the door to create a wall of glass rather than a solid barrier. The result is a room with a bright, spacious feeling.

FABULOUS FRENCH DOORS

Patio doors come in two styles, French and sliding. They affect a room the same way a window does, only they take it one step farther—they open a portion of a wall and provide a gateway to the great outdoors.

Traditional French doors are hinged and swing either in or out. These doors need ample room to swing freely. French doors also come in sliding versions where one panel is stationary and the other slides. The sliding versions use space more efficiently and are easier to weatherproof.

A formal French door is the centerpiece of this stately window presentation. A formal window dressing uses a fabric-covered rod as if it were a thin cornice, separating the transom windows and giving them an almost clerestory look. The thick drapes help create a more intimate setting.

Vertical blinds and a fabric-covered tubal cornice dress this French door. The vertical blinds and the top treatment have a contemporary design that complements the modern look of the door.

Traditional French doors swing open to guide you onto the outside patio. Transom windows with decorative trim are incorporated into the distinctive doors.

SPECTACULAR SLIDING DOORS

Sliding patio doors don't require the space for door swing that French doors do. They seal tightly and are easier to weatherproof. It's also easy to incorporate a screen into a sliding patio door.

Sliding patio doors expand the space in a room by opening to eliminate the wall that divides the room from the outdoor living area. Even when closed, patio doors and their transparent glass panes make the room seem larger and more spacious.

Photo courtesy of Hurd Millwork Co.

This French-style patio door is fashioned with attractive muntins to match a large neighboring window. The sliding door allows easy access from inside the house to the sunny poolside area.

Photo courtesy of Loewen Windows

A sliding patio door is the center of this spacious window display. The door and surrounding windows visually and physically link and expand the kitchen area to the deck outside.

Photo courtesy of Andersen Windows

Photo courtesy of ADO Corporation

A sleek, sliding patio door is topped with a narrow awning window. The simple but effective window design brings breezes and bright light into this dark entryway. The large glass area opens the space to the deck outside.

Traditional drapes and sheer curtains conceal a sliding door in this formal living room. When the curtains are open, the large glass doors flood the room with natural light and connect it with area outside.

Even the pet parrot feels upstaged by the brilliant colors used in this imaginative window presentation. Three swinging French doors joined side-by-side create a beautiful glass wall that can be completely opened to connect the indoors with the patio just outside. Large window areas can handle large window treatments, and the combination used here is a perfect example. Purple and gold are the unifying colors in this drapery ensemble. Sheer white curtains are hung in the center of each door and tied back to open up the room. They can be easily closed for privacy. Thick columns and a scalloped cornice are wrapped in drapery fabric to create a spiral striped frame that encompasses all three windows. Luxurious long drapes are mounted behind the cornice and hang between the windows, gracefully flowing to the floor.

CREATIVE COMBINATIONS

Joining several windows together to form incredible combinations can be a beautifully effective way to solve a number of problems with one window design. Variables like light, air circulation and space constraints can all be managed with an effective window plan.

For as many different window combinations as you can imagine, there are twice as many window treatment combinations you can use to dress them. Today's interiors are pushing the envelope of the imagination and almost anything goes—as long as you can live with it.

A dramatic window dressing has as much impact as a dramatic window display. This original design combines three formal window treatments to create an artistic statement. A fabric-covered box cornice is the core of this drapery design. It hangs from a decorative pole along with lustrous long pleated drapes and two small valances that are cut to follow the sculpted curve of the cornice. The highlight of the design is a single large swag, made of light, sheer fabric, meticulously pleated and tied to one side.

Photos courtesy of ADO Corporation

Photo courtesy of Kolbe & Kolbe Millwork Co.

Plush red velvet drapes are topped by fringed red velvet swags that are uniformly draped across a pole. A white cloud curtain hangs behind the red velvet and creates a soft, billowy textured backdrop.

Photo courtesy of Spring Window Fashions

A satiny curtain panel, a swingy swag and a custom-colored blind are combined to create this eclectic dressing design. Fancy swag holders and gold fringe are ornate details that give a finished look to the top treatment.

A classic window combination was custom-styled to follow the cut of the outside of this stucco home. A large Palladian window is flanked by two tall, narrow sidelights and incorporates decorative muntins to reinforce the definitive shape of the window's design.

Sometimes less is best. This simple combination dresses an ordinary casement window with a fancy three-tiered cornice and the classic, clean look of two narrow, white pleated shades.

LIST OF CONTRIBUTORS

We'd like to thank the following companies for providing the photographs used in this book:

ADO Corporation
P.O. Box 3447
Spartenburg, SC 29304
1-800-845-0918

Andersen Window Corporation
Bayport, MN 55003
1-800-426-4261

Architectural Components Inc.
26 North Leverett Road
Montague, MA 01351
413-367-9441
fax 413-367-9461

Conrad Imports
575 Tenth Street
San Francisco, CA 94103-4829
415-626-3303

Crestline Windows & Doors
SNE Enterprises
One Wausau Center
Wausau, WI 54402-8007
715-845-1161

Devenco Products
2688 East Ponce De Leon Avenue
Decatur, GA 30030
1-800-888-4597

Eagle Window and Door, Inc.
375 East 9th
P.O. Box 1072
Dubuque, IA 52004-1072
319-556-2270

Hurd Millwork Company
P.O. Box 319
Medford, WI 54451
715-748-2011

Kolbe & Kolbe
1323 South 11th Avenue
Wausaw, WI 54401
715-842-5666

Loewen Windows
Box 2260
Steinbach, Manitoba
Canada ROA2A0
1-800-563-9367

Marvin Windows & Doors
P.O. Box 100
Warroad, MN 56763
1-800-346-5128

Phifer Wire Products, Inc.
P.O. Box 1700
Tuscaloosa, AL 35403-1700
1-800-874-3007

Magnolia Shutters
a Division of Rushman Industries
2929 Irving Blvd
Dallas, TX 75247
214-943-1000

Simpson Door Company
P.O. Box 210
McCleary, WA 98557
206-495-3291

VETTER
SNE Enterprises
One Wausau Center
Wausau, WI 54402-8007
715-845-1161

Springs Window Fashions
7549 Graber Road
Middleton, WI 53562-1096

Stelz Studios
Fine Leaded Glass Windows & Lamps
98 Stanton Station Road
Flemington, NJ 08822
908-806-7023

Wenco Windows
A division of JELD-WEN
335 Commerce Drive
Mt. Vernon, OH 43050-4643
614-397-3403